Da'thy's
Healthy Cuisine

Dorothy Woods

GoToPublish LLC
1-888-337-1724
www.gotopublish.com
info@gotopublish.com

CONTENTS

DEDICATION

This book is dedicated to my executive assistant Ryan Wiggan, who has worked with me for the past 10 years. His self-discipline in his eating habits has had a profound effect upon me. I trust that these healthy delicacies will add to the quality of your life.

APPETIZERS

BAKED ROSTI POTATOES

2 tablespoons oil
2 packages (20 oz.) hash brown, shredded
1 ½ cups cheddar cheese, shredded
½ cup flour
1 small onions, grated
1 egg, beaten

Instructions:
Preheat oven 400°F. Brush oil onto bottom and up sides of a 13x9 baking dish. Combine all remaining ingredients except egg. Add egg. Mix lightly and press into bottom of baking dish. Bake 60 minutes or until golden brown. Let stand 10 minutes before cutting to serve.

Serves 4.

EASY BISCUIT AND GRAVY

1 pound ground sausage
8 prepared biscuits
¼ cup all-purpose flour
2 cups milk
salt and pepper to taste

Instructions:
Crumble and cook sausage in large skillet over medium heat until browned. Stir in flour until dissolved. Gradually stir in milk. Cook gravy until thick and bubbly. Season with salt and pepper. Serve hot over biscuits.

Serves 4.

EASY OVEN ROASTED POTATOES

5 pounds baking potatoes, peeled & cubed
2 teaspoons salt
1 teaspoon pepper
1 stick unsalted butter, melted

Instructions:
Preheat oven to 425°F. In large bowl mix butter, salt, and pepper. Add potatoes and toss. Place potatoes on a 9x13 pan in a single layer. Shake pan (mix and turn) occasionally. Bake approximately 45 Minutes.

Serves 4.

SPINACH FRITTATA

3 tablespoons olive oil
1 small garlic clove, crushed
10 eggs
1 cup raw spinach, finely chopped
⅓ cup Parmesan cheese, grated
1 tablespoon chopped parsley
1 tablespoon salt
¼ teaspoon pepper

Instructions:
Preheat oven to 350°F. Heat oil in 10-inch heavy skillet with heat-resistant handle. Add onion; sauté until onion is tender and golden brown; about 5 minutes. In large bowl, combine remaining ingredients. With wire whisk or fork, beat until well blended.

Turn into skillet, with onion. Cook over low heat, 3 minutes, lifting bottom with spatula as eggs set. Bake uncovered, 10 minutes, or until top is set. With spatula, loosen from bottom and around edges, and slide onto serving platter. Cut into wedges.

Serves 4.

STUFFED MUSHROOM

12 medium mushrooms
2 tablespoons diet margarine
¼ cup green peppers, finely chopped
1 teaspoon salt
¼ cup onions, finely chopped
dash of pepper

Instructions:

Preheat oven to 350°F. Wipe mushrooms with damp cloth. Remove stems; chop stems finely. Heat 1 tablespoon margarine in large skillet. Sauté mushroom caps; on bottom only, 3 minutes; remove. Arrange, rounded side down, in shallow baking pan.

Heat rest of margarine in same skillet. Sauté stems, green pepper, and onion until tender; about 5 minutes. Season with salt and pepper; remove from heat. Spoon mixture into mushroom caps. Bake 15 minutes, or until heated through.

Serves 4.

SWEET POTATO BISCUITS

2 cups all-purpose flour
1 teaspoon salt
¾ cup buttermilk
1 cup mashed sweet potato
½ teaspoon baking soda
½ cup butter flavoured Crisco, melted
2 tablespoons brown sugar, firmly packed
1 tablespoon baking powder

Instructions:
Heat oven to 425°F. Combine flour, baking powder, and salt in large bowl. Combine sweet potato, brown sugar, and butter flavoured Crisco.

Beat at low speed of electric mixer until well blended and fluffy. Dissolve baking soda in buttermilk. Stir buttermilk and sweet potato mixture alternately into dry ingredients. Roll dough ½ inch thick.

Cut with floured 2-inch round cutter. Place on ungreased baking sheet. Bake at 425°F for 20 minutes. Make 12 to 16 biscuits.

Serves 4.

ZUCCHINI WITH CHEESE

1 ½ pounds zucchini
¼ cup olive oil
¼ cup all-purpose flour
1 ½ teaspoons salt
1 ½ teaspoons dried oregano
¼ teaspoon pepper
2 medium tomatoes, sliced
1 cup sour cream
½ cup Parmesan cheese, grated

Instructions:
Preheat oven to 350°F. Lightly grease 8-by-8-by-2-inch baking dish. With stiff brush, scrub zucchini well. Cut crosswise into ¼-inch slices. In medium bowl, combine flour with 1/2 teaspoon salt, ½ teaspoon oregano, and ⅛ teaspoon pepper.

Toss zucchini slices in seasoned flour, to coat them well. Slowly heat oil in large, heavy skillet. Sauté zucchini until golden brown; about 4 minutes on each side. Drain. Cover bottom of baking dish with zucchini. Top with tomato slices.

Combine sour cream, rest of salt, oregano, and pepper, and spread evenly over tomato slices. Then sprinkle with grated cheese. Bake 30 minutes, or until cheese is melted and zucchini is tender.

CASSEROLES

CHEESE AND RICE CASSEROLE

¼ cup butter
1 cup onions, chopped
3 cans (4-oz. size) green chilies, drained and halved
lengthwise, leaving seeds
4 cups freshly cooked white rice
1 cup cream-style cottage cheese
2 cups natural cheddar cheese, grated
⅛ teaspoon pepper
½ teaspoon salt
2 cups sour cream
1 large bay leaves, crumbled
1 chopped parsley

Instructions:
Preheat oven to 375°F. Lightly grease 12-by-8-by 2-inch, 2-quart baking dish. In hot butter in large skillet, sauté onion until golden; about 5 minutes. Remove from heat. Stir in hot rice, sour cream, cottage cheese, bay leaf, salt, and pepper; toss lightly to mix well. Layer half the rice mixture in bottom of baking dish; top with half of chilies; sprinkle with half of cheese.

Repeat. Bake, uncovered, 25 minutes, or until bubbly and hot. Sprinkle with chopped parsley.

Serves 4.

CHICKEN AND SWISS CASSEROLE

4 cups chicken, cooked and chopped
2 cups croutons
1 ½ cups Swiss cheese, shredded
⅔ cup mayonnaise
½ cup milk
¼ cup onions, chopped
4 celery stalks, sliced

Instructions:
Preheat oven to 350°F. Combine all ingredients. Spoon into 2 quart casserole. Bake 40 minutes or until heated through.

Serves 4.

CHICKEN CASSEROLE

4 skinless, boneless chicken breast halves
1 can (10.75) cream of chicken soup
1 cup sour cream
32 buttery round crackers
¼ cup onions, chopped
¼ cup mushrooms, chopped

Instructions:
Preheat oven 350°F. Boil chicken 30 minutes, until cooked through. Chop into bite size pieces and place in a 9x13 baking dish. Combine soup, sour cream, onion and mushrooms. Pour mixture over chicken and top with crumbled crackers. Cover and bake for 30 minutes.

Serves 4.

CURRIED FISH CASSEROLE

1 tablespoon butter
1 ½ cups onions, sliced
2 teaspoons curry powder
1 package frozen fish fillet of your choice, unthawed
1 can (8 ¼ oz.) tomatoes, drained
½ teaspoon salt to taste
⅛ teaspoon pepper
1 chopped parsley
1 large apple, cored and thinly sliced

Instructions:

In hot butter in large, non-stick skillet with tight-fitting cover, sauté onions until soft; about 5 minutes. Add curry powder. Cook, stirring, 5 minutes longer. Cut frozen fillets crosswise into 1-inch strips. Arrange fish fillets in bottom of casserole. Place onions on top of fish; top with apples and tomatoes. Sprinkle with salt and pepper.

Cook over medium heat, covered, 10 minutes. To serve: sprinkle liberally with parsley.

Serves 4.

HOT CHICKEN SALAD CASSEROLE

4 cups chicken breasts, cooked & shredded
2 cans (10.75) cream of chicken soup
2 cups celery, chopped
2 cans water chestnuts, diced
1 cup mayonnaise
1 ½ cups cheddar cheese, shredded
1 teaspoon salt
1 small bag potato chips

Instructions:
Preheat oven 350°F. Combine first 8 ingredients and crumble potato chips on top. Bake for 45 minutes.

Serves 4.

LAMB AND VEGETABLE CASSEROLE

2 tablespoons salad oil
2 pounds lamb shoulder, cut in 1-inch cubes
2 medium onions, sliced
1 clove garlic, crushed
½ cup raw regular white rice
1 pound potatoes, pared and very thinly sliced
4 teaspoons salt
1 ½ teaspoons curry powder
¼ teaspoon pepper
½ pound zucchini, sliced
1 package (9 oz.) frozen artichoke hearts
2 cans tomatoes, un-drained
1 parsley, chopped

Instructions:
Preheat oven to 350°F. In hot oil in large skillet, sauté lamb cubes, a third at a time, until browned wee on all sides; about 20 minutes in all. Remove lamb as it browns.

Add onion and garlic to drippings in skillet; sauté until golden; about 5 minutes. Return lamb cubes to skillet, mixing well. In 3-quart casserole, place in layers, a third of meat mixture, rice, potatoes, salt, curry powder, pepper, zucchini, artichoke hearts, and tomatoes. Repeat layering twice with rest of these ingredients. Bake, covered, 1 ½ hours, or until lamb and potatoes are tender. To serve; sprinkle top with parsley.

Serves 4.

SEAFOOD MINI-CASSEROLES

5 tablespoons butter
3 tablespoons flour
½ teaspoon mustard, dry
2 pounds cooked, shelled, deveined shrimp
2 cans (5 oz.) lobster meat
2 cans (7 ½ oz.) king crab meat
3 egg yolks
2 cups heavy cream
6 tablespoons Madeira wine
¼ teaspoon salt
¼ teaspoon pepper
1 dash cayenne pepper
1 cup milk

Instructions:

Melt butter in large, heavy saucepan. Remove from heat. Sift in flour, mustard, salt, and pepper until smooth. Gradually add milk, stirring constantly. Bring to boiling, stirring constantly; cook, stirring, 1 minute. Remove from heat. In small bowl, slightly beat egg yolks with cream and wine; gradually stir into hot mixture. Cook over low heat, stirring constantly, until hot but not boiling. Stir in shrimp, lobster, and crab; cook over low heat until very hot (do not boil.) Serve over hot cooked rice in individual casseroles, or in patty shells.

Serves 4.

SUMMER SQUASH CASSEROLE

1 package (8 oz.) herb seasoned stuffing mix
½ cup onions, chopped
1 can (10 ¾ oz.) condensed cream of chicken soup
1 cup sour cream
1 cup carrots, shredded
½ cup butter, melted
2 pounds zucchini or yellow squash, about 6 cups
salt to taste

Instructions:
Heat oven to 350°F. Combine squash and onion in large saucepan. Cover with water. Season with salt. Cook 5 minutes. Drain.

Combine soup and sour cream in large bowl. Stir in carrots. Fold in squash and onions. Combine stuffing mix and butter. Spread half into bottom of 12 x 7 ½ x2 inch baking dish. Spoon in vegetable mixture.

Sprinkle with remaining stuffing. Bake at 350°F for 30 minutes or until heated thoroughly.

Serves 4.

TOMATO-ONION-CHEESE CASSEROLE

4 cups onions, thinly sliced
4 medium ripe tomatoes, peeled & sliced
1 teaspoon salt
¼ teaspoon pepper
½ cup bread crumbs
3 tablespoons butter
½ teaspoon basil leaves, dried
6 slices American cheese

Instructions:
Preheat oven to 350°F. Lightly grease 1 ½ quart casserole. In 1 inch of boiling water in medium saucepan, cook onion, covered, 10 minutes, drain. In prepared casserole, layer, in order, half of tomatoes and onion.

Sprinkle with half of salt, pepper, and basil. Top with half of cheese. Repeat. Toss bread crumbs with melted butter, and sprinkle over top of cheese. Bake, uncovered, 30 minutes, or until tomatoes are tender.

Da'thy's Healthy Cuisine

CHEESE

COTTAGE CHEESE IN TOMATOES

3 medium tomatoes
1 (12 oz.) diet creamed cottage cheese
⅓ cup as oil, pared & grated
1 tablespoon Italian-style dressing, low-calorie
⅓ cup green onions, finely chopped
4 radishes, coarsely grated
¼ teaspoon salt
1 crisp lettuce
⅓ cup cucumbers, diced and pared
1 parsley or dill sprigs

Instructions:

Cut tomatoes in half crosswise. With spoon, scoop out pulp and seeds; drain. In medium bowl, combine cottage cheese, carrot, cucumber, onion, radishes, drained tomato pulp, salt, and dressing; mix lightly.

Spoon into tomatoes. Arrange on lettuce on salad plates. Garnish with fresh parsley or dill sprigs.

COOKIES

GINGER COOKIES

⅔ cup shortening
1 egg, beaten
2 cups flour
1 teaspoon salt
1 teaspoon ground cloves
1 cup sugar
¼ cup light molasses
1 teaspoon baking soda
1 teaspoon ginger
1 teaspoon ground cumin

Instructions:
Preheat oven 350°F. Cream shortening, egg, sugar, and molasses. Mix all dry ingredient together and add to shortening mix. Do not add too much flour. Roll out on cutting board. Cut to size desired. Bake for 15 minutes.

Serves 4.

PEANUT BUTTER COOKIES

1 cup peanut butter, smooth or chunky
1 cup granulated sugar
1 large egg

Instructions:

Preheat oven to 350°F. Mix the three ingredients together until smooth. Drop using teaspoon, onto cookie sheet 2-inches apart. If desired, roll in some sugar before placing on cookie sheet. Press with folk and press again in opposite direction. Bake 12 minutes. Do not brown, do not over bake.

DAIRY

THE TRIDENT'S SPECIAL HEALTH SHAKE

1 cup crushed ice
1 cup yogurt
¼ cup honey
1 cup cantaloupe, cut-up
1 fresh mint leaves
1 tablespoon wheat germ
½ cup fresh papaya, cut-up
2 tablespoons raw sugar
½ cup fresh strawberries sliced or
½ pkg (10-oz.) frozen sliced strawberries, thawed

Instructions:
In blender, combine half of all ingredients and blend until smooth. Turn into chilled pitcher. Blend remainder of ingredient and add to pitcher. To serve, pour into chilled glasses. Garnish with mint.

DESSERTS

BUTTERMILK HUSH PUPPIES

1 cup yellow cornmeal
1 ½ teaspoons baking soda
1 cup buttermilk
¼ cup onions, finely chopped
½ cup all-purpose flour
½ teaspoon salt
1 egg, beaten

Instructions:

Heat 3 inches oil in 365°F in deep fryer or deep saucepan. Combine cornmeal, flour, baking soda, and salt and pepper in large bowl. Stir in buttermilk, egg, and onion.

Mix well. Drop be teaspoonful, a few at a time, into oil. Fry 2 minutes or until dark brown.

Turn as needed for even browning. Remove with slotted metal spoon. Drain on paper towel.

Serves 4.

DOUBLE STRAWBERRY DESSERT

1 package (10 oz.) frozen strawberries, thawed
1 envelope low-calorie strawberry-flavoured gelatin
1 egg white
1 granulated sugar

Instructions:

Drain liquid from strawberries into 2-cup measure. Add water to make 2 cups. In small saucepan, bring to boiling. Pour over gelatine in medium bowl, stirring until gelatine is dissolved. Refrigerate, stirring occasionally, just until consistency of unbeaten egg white. Gently fold drained strawberries into gelatine mixture. Dip rims of 4 stemmed glasses into egg white, then into granulated sugar. Spoon strawberry mixture into stemmed glasses. Refrigerate dessert, in glasses, for several hours, or until it is firm.

Serves 4.

EASY APPLE BREAD

1 ½ cups oil
1 teaspoon vanilla extract
1 teaspoon cinnamon
4 eggs
½ teaspoon salt
2 cups sugar
3 cups flour
3 cups apples, chopped
1 teaspoon baking soda
nuts (optional)

Instructions:

Preheat oven to 350°F. Cream together oil, eggs, and sugar. Add remaining ingredients and mix. Lightly grease two loaf pans, splitting batter between two pans. Bake for 70 Minutes.

Serves 4.

FRIED APPLE TURNOVERS

⅔ cup sugar
½ teaspoon cinnamon
¼ cup butter
2 cups tart apples, pared and sliced
1 package refrigerator biscuits
icing sugar for sprinkle

Instructions:
Combine first 4 ingredients in a saucepan. Simmer mixture, stirring it occasionally until the apples are tender. Separate the biscuits and roll each to an oval shape, about 5-inches long. Place 1 tablespoon of the apple filling on ½ of the oval, then fold the dough over the filling and seal the edges with a folk (be sure they are well sealed or the filling will leak out).

Fry the turnovers in hot 375°F oil for about 1 minute or until golden brown, turning them once. Drain on paper towels and sprinkle with icing sugar. Serve warm.

Serves 4.

FUDGE BROWNIES

2 eggs
1 teaspoon baking powder
2 cups sugar
½ teaspoon salt
1 ½ cups flour
½ cup oil
1 teaspoon vanilla extract
½ cup cocoa
4 tablespoons water

Instructions:
Preheat oven to 325°F. Combine oil and cocoa. Slightly beat eggs, water and vanilla.

Mix (don't beat) cocoa and oil into egg mixture. Add sugar. Add flour, baking powder and salt to the mixture. Grease and flour 9x13 baking pan. Bake for 20 minutes.

Serves 4.

PEACHES WITH YOGURT

1 can diet peaches, drained
½ container (8 oz. size) plain yogurt
1 tablespoon sugar
1 dash almond extract

Instructions:
Arrange peaches in small glass serving bowl. Combine yogurt, sugar, and almond extract; blend well with rubber scraper.

Pour over peaches. Refrigerate at least 2 hours, until very well chilled.

Serves 4.

PINEAPPLE-PEACH MELBA

1 quart vanilla ice cream, softened
1 can (8 ½ oz.) crushed pineapple, well drained
1 package (10 oz.) frozen raspberries, thawed and un-drained
¼ cup brandy
3 peaches, fresh

Instructions:
In chilled large bowl of electric mixer, at low speed, beat ice cream just until mushy.

Quickly stir in pineapple until well combined with ice cream. Turn mixture into 8-by-8-by 2-inch pan. Cover with foil. Freeze mixture until firm, several hours or overnight. Wash and peel peaches. Cut peaches in half: remove pits. Place peach halves in medium bowl; sprinkle with brandy. Press raspberries and juice through sieve, to make puree; pour over peaches.

Refrigerate, covered, several hours or overnight. To serve: With slotted utensil, remove peach halves to individual serving plates. Place scoop of pineapple ice cream in center of each peach half: spoon raspberry sauce over top.

Serves 4.

SKILLET FUDGE

2 tablespoons cocoa
2 tablespoons corn syrup
1 ½ cups granulated sugar
1 teaspoon vanilla extract
4 tablespoons butter
7 tablespoons milk

Instructions:

Combine all ingredients in heavy skillet. Bring to a boil and boil for 1 minute (test for soft ball in cold water) Cool for 5 minutes.

Beat until it loses its gloss (about 5 minutes). Pour into greased 8-inch pan.

Cool and cut into squares.

Serves 4.

SWEET POTATO MUFFINS

1 cup skim or low fat milk
1 tablespoon molasses
½ cup cold mashed sweet potatoes or yams
½ cup brown sugar, firmly packed
1 egg
3 tablespoons oil
1 teaspoon orange peels, grated
1 cup all-purpose flour
½ cup whole wheat flour
½ cup oat bran
2 ½ teaspoons baking powder

Instructions:

Heat oven to 400°F. Grease twelve medium (About 2 ½ inch) muffin cups or use paper or foil liners. Combine milk, sweet potatoes, brown sugar, egg, oil, and molasses in large bowl. Stir until well mixed. Combine all-purpose flour, whole wheat flour, oat bran, baking powder and orange peel. Add to liquid mixture. Stir just until dry ingredients are moistened. Spoon batter into muffin cups. Bake at 400°F for 25 minutes.

DRESSINGS

LOW-CALORIE ONION SOUP DIP

1 cup yogurt
1 cup diet cottage cheese
3 tablespoons onion soup mix, dry
¼ teaspoon chili powder

Instructions:

In medium bowl, combine yogurt and cottage cheese until well blended. Stir in dry onion-soup mix and chili powder.

Refrigerate dip, covered, 3 hours, to chill well and to let flavour develop. Arrange on tray with an assortment of crisp vegetables and chilled shrimp.

Serves 4.

SHRIMP LOUIS DRESSING

1 cup mayonnaise
¾ teaspoon horseradish, prepared
2 pounds shrimp, shelled, deveined, and cooked
½ cup chili sauce
1 tablespoon chopped parsley
1 crisp Boston lettuce, to make 6 lettuce cups
¾ teaspoon Worcestershire sauce
1 watercress sprigs
1 tablespoon onions, grated

Instructions:

Make dressing: In medium bowl, combine mayonnaise, chili sauce, Worcestershire, grated onion, parsley, and horseradish.

Beat with rotary beater until smooth and well combined. Refrigerate covered, several hours, until very well chilled.

To serve:

Arrange lettuce cups on individual luncheon plates. Chop shrimp coarsely. Divide evenly into lettuce cups. Spoon some of dressing over shrimp. Pass rest of dressing in serving boat. Garnish each plate with watercress sprigs.

CAKES

BLUEBERRY TEA CAKE

1 egg, beaten
⅔ cup sugar
1 ½ cups cake flour, sifted
½ teaspoon cinnamon
¾ teaspoon salt
⅓ cup milk
3 tablespoons butter, melted
1 teaspoon vanilla extract
1 cup fresh blueberries
2 tablespoons sugar

Instructions:

Preheat oven to 400°F. Grease 1 ½ quart, shallow baking dish. In medium bowl, with wooden spoon, beat egg. Gradually beat in ⅔ cup sugar; beat until well combined.

Sift together flour, baking powder, cinnamon, and salt. Add to sugar mixture alternately with milk. Beat well after each addition.

Add butter and vanilla. Beat thoroughly. Fold in blueberries. Pour batter into prepared pan. Sprinkle top with 2 tablespoons sugar. Bake 30 minutes, or until top springs back when lightly touched with fingertip. Serve warm, with butter.

Serves 4.

COLD OVEN POUND CAKE

1 (18 oz.) box golden cake mix, butter recipe
1 cup sugar
1 cup flour
1 cup oil
6 eggs
1 cup sour cream

Instructions:
Mix sugar, flour, and oil. Add cake mix. Add eggs one at a time and beat for two (2) minutes. Add sour cream, pour into Bundt pan. Cook for 60 minutes at 350°F.

Serves 5.

LOW-CALORIE SPONGE CAKE

½ cup reconstituted non-fat dry milk
1 cup all-purpose flour, sifted
1 ½ teaspoons baking powder
2 teaspoons lemon peels, grated
1 dash salt
3 eggs
¾ cup sugar

Instructions:
In small saucepan, heat milk until bubbles form around edge of pan. Remove from heat; set aside. Preheat oven to 350°F. Sift flour with baking powder and salt; set aside. In small bowl of electric mixer, at high speed, beat eggs until thick and lemon-coloured. Gradually add sugar, beating until mixture is smooth and well blended; about 5 minutes. At low speed, blend in flour mixture just until smooth. Add warm milk and peel, beating just until combined.

Immediately pour batter into ungreased, 9-inch angel food pan. Bake 30 minutes, or until cake tester inserted in center comes out clean. Invert pan over neck or bottle; let cool completely. Serve plain.

Serves 4.

WALNUT RAISIN CAKE

1 ½ cups brown sugar, packed
½ cup liquid margarine
2 eggs
1 teaspoon vanilla extract
2 cups apples, pared & finely chopped
½ teaspoon baking powder
1 teaspoon cinnamon
½ cup milk
1 cup walnuts, chopped
¾ cup flour, unsifted
1 cup raisins
¾ teaspoon baking soda

Instructions:
Preheat oven to 350°F. Grease and flour 13-by-9-by-2-inch pan. In large bowl, combine sugar and margarine. Using wooden spoon, beat in eggs and vanilla.

Sift flour with soda, baking powder, and cinnamon. Stir into egg mixture, alternately with milk. Stir in apples, chopped nuts, and raisins. Turn into prepared pan. Bake 45 minutes, until surface springs back when gently pressed with fingertip. Let cool in pan on wire. Frost, if desired. Cut into 20 squares. Top each with walnut.

FISH

LEMON BAKED FISH

1 pound frozen fish fillet of your choice
2 tablespoons olive oil
3 tablespoons lemon juice
1 fresh dill
salt and pepper to taste

Instructions:
Preheat oven 350°F. Oil a baking dish and arrange fish in a single layer. Season with a little salt and pepper. Add a few drops of olive oil and pour the lemon juice over.

Scatter dill on top for flavour. Bake the fish for 30 minutes. Serve with juices from the pan.

Serves 4.

PARMESAN BAKED FISH

¼ cup mayonnaise
2 tablespoons parmesan cheese, grated
⅛ teaspoon cayenne pepper
2 teaspoons lemon juice
10 butter crackers, crushed
1 pound salmon or cod fillets

Instructions:
Preheat oven to 350°F.

Mix mayo, cheese, and cayenne pepper until well blended. Place salmon or cod on foil-lined shallow

Baking pan. Drizzle evenly with lemon juice. Top with cheese mixture and spread evenly to cover salmon or cod. Sprinkle with butter cracker crumbs. Bake 42-15 minutes or until salmon or cod flakes easily with folk and crumbs are golden brown.

MEATS

AVOCADO MEAT LOAF

¾ cup celery, diced
½ cup green onions, minced
2 tablespoons parsley, minced
½ cup green peppers
1 pound ground veal
1 pound hamburgers
1 (8 oz.) can tomato sauce
1 cup bread crumbs
2 cups fresh chopped mushrooms
1 egg, slightly beaten
2 tablespoons flour
1 large avocados, skinned & diced
2 teaspoons celery salt
½ teaspoon pepper

Instructions:

Fry 4 strips bacon until crisp and remove from pan. In same fat, sauté ¾ cup diced celery, ½ cup minced green onions, 2 tablespoon minced parsley, and ½ cup diced green pepper. When done, remove to a large bowl.

Add: 1 lb. ground veal; 1 egg, slightly beaten; 1 Ib. hamburger, 2 tablespoons flour 1 8-oz. can tomato sauce; 1 large avocado, skinned and diced; 1 cup bread crumbs; 2 teaspoons celery salt; 2 cups fresh chopped mushrooms; ½ teaspoon pepper.

Pack into a 5x5x9-inch loaf pan, sprinkle generously with paprika, and bake at 350°F for 45 minutes. Remove excess fat from pan and bake for 45 minutes more.

Serves 4.

BACON WRAP DATES

6 pieces thinly sliced bacon
18 pitted dates

Instructions:
Cut bacon slices crosswise into about 4-inch lengths. Wrap a piece snugly around each date, overlapping ends. Set dates, seam sides down, in a 10 or 12-inch non-stick frying pan over medium heat (may have to fry dates in batches). Turn dates occasionally until bacon is browned and crisp on all sides, 10 minutes total. Transfer dates to paper towels to drain and blot dry.

Serve warm or cool.

Serves 4.

BRAISED BEEF WITH CABBAGE

2 tablespoons salad oil
1 ½ pounds beef chuck, cut into 1 ½-inch cubes
2 onions, sliced
1 apple, pared, cored, & thinly sliced
4 medium potatoes, pared & quartered lengthwise
1 head green cabbage, washed and cut in 8 wedges
2 teaspoons sugar
2 teaspoons salt
⅛ teaspoon pepper
2 cans tomatoes, un-drained

Instructions:
Heat oil in large skillet. Add beef, and brown on all sides. Remove. Add onions to skillet, and cook slowly until golden brown. Add browned beef. Stir in 1 cup water. Add apple and tomatoes, then sprinkle with sugar, salt, and pepper. Bring to boiling; reduce heat, and simmer, covered, 2 hours. Add potatoes and cabbage to meat mixture; simmer, covered, 30 minutes longer, or until vegetables are tender.

Serves 4.

BRAISED LAMB SHANKS

4 lamb shanks
1 ½ teaspoons unseasoned instant meat tenderizer
2 chicken bouillon cubes
2 cups boiling water
½ pound white onion, peeled
2 stalks celery
1 bay leaves
1 teaspoon paprika
½ teaspoon salt
½ teaspoon pepper
1 pound carrots

Instructions:
Preheat oven to 325°F. Wipe lamb shanks with damp paper towels. Trim off and fat. Sprinkle shanks with meat tenderizer. In non-stick Dutch oven, over medium heat, brown shanks on all sides, turning with tongs, 15 to 20 minutes. Dissolve bouillon cubes in boiling water; pour over shanks.

Add onions, bay leaf, paprika, salt and pepper. Bake, covered, 1 hour.

Meanwhile, pare carrots. Cut celery into 1-inch pieces. Add vegetables to Dutch oven. Bake, covered, 60 minutes longer, or until vegetables and meat are tender.

Serves 4.

CALIFORNIA MEAT LOAF

1 pound hamburgers
1 cup corn flakes
2 eggplants, peeled, slightly beaten
1 teaspoon salt
⅛ teaspoon pepper
½ cup milk
¼ cup catsup
1 tablespoon Worcestershire sauce
1 cup raisins
⅓ cup cheddar cheese, grated

Instructions:
MIX

1 Ib. hamburger; ½ cup milk

1 cup corn flakes; ¼ cup catsup

2 eggs, slightly beaten; 1 tablespoons

Worcestershire sauce; 1 teaspoon salt;

1 cup raisins; ⅛ teaspoon pepper

Shape into loaf. Sprinkle ⅓ cup grated cheddar cheese over top. Bake 350°F for 1 hour.

Serves 4.

CRAB IMPERIAL

1 egg
1 tablespoon capers, drained
⅓ cup mayonnaise
2 tablespoons green peppers, chopped
2 teaspoons Worcestershire sauce
1 tablespoon lemon juice
2 cans (7 ¾ oz.) king crab meat
1 cup cheddar cheese, grated
2 slices white bread, cubed
⅛ teaspoon dry mustard

Instructions:

Preheat oven to 400°F. In medium bowl, combine egg; mayonnaise, dry mustard, Worcestershire sauce, and lemon juice; mix well. Remove any cartilage and shell from crab meat. (If canned crab is used, drain thoroughly.) Add crab meat to egg mixture with capers, green pepper, and bread cubes. Toss lightly with fork until well combined.

Divide crab meat mixture into 4 individual scallops' shells, or turn into shallow, 1-quart baking dish. Bake 10 minutes. Sprinkle cheese over top. Bake 5 minutes longer, or until cheese is melted and bubbly. Serve garnished with lemon wedges.

Serves 4.

CRUSTY MEAT LOAF

1 ½ pounds hamburgers
1 eggs, slightly beaten
½ cup bread crumbs
½ cup catsup
½ cup water
1 ½ teaspoons salt
2 tablespoons onions, chopped
1 ½ cups buttered bread cubes

Instructions:
MIX:

1 ½ lbs hamburger, ½ cup water

1 egg, slightly beaten; 2 tablespoon chopped onion; ½ cup bread crumbs, 1 ½ teaspoon salt; ½ cup catsup

Form into loaf and gently press 1 ½ cups buttered bread cubes into top of loaf. Bake at 350°F for 1 hour.

Serves 4.

DIETETIC MEAT LOAF

1 pound lean hamburger
1 egg, slightly beaten
⅓ cup onions, minced
¾ teaspoon salt
¼ teaspoon pepper
½ cup chili sauce
½ cup condensed beef bouillon
½ cup non-fat skimmed milk

Instructions:
Soften 2 slices well-browned toast in ½ cup non-fat skimmed milk.

Add:

1 Ib. lean hamburger; ¾ teaspoon salt

1 egg, slightly beaten; ¼ teaspoon pepper

⅓ cup minced onion

Form into a loaf and place in the center of a baking dish. Top with ½ cup chili sauce and pour ½ cup condensed beef bouillon around loaf. Bake at 350°F for 1 ½ hours.

Serves 4.

FIVE-FLAVOR BEEF

¼ cup olive oil
4 pounds boned chuck or rump pot roast
½ cup soy sauce
4 stick cinnamon
2 anise seeds
½ cup sugar
1 cup sherry
3 tablespoons cornstarch

Instructions:
Slowly heat oil in Dutch oven. Add meat, and brown well on all sides; about 15 minutes. Meanwhile, combine soy sauce, 2 cups water, cinnamon stack, anise seeds, and sugar. Pour over meat. Simmer, covered, 3 hours, or until meat is tender. (After first 2 hours of cooking time, add sherry.) Remove meat to heated platter.

Reserve 2 ½ cups liquid in Dutch oven, and discard rest. Bring to boiling. Meanwhile, in small bowl, make smooth mixture of cornstarch and ½ cup water. Stir into boiling in Dutch oven. Simmer, stirring, until thickened and translucent. Serve over beef.

Serves 4.

ITALIAN PORK CHOP

1 ½ bone in pork chops, 3/4 inch thick
1 cup light balsamic vinaigrette dressing
1 package (16 oz.) frozen mixed vegetables
1 teaspoon oregano, dried
1 (14.5 oz.) can Italian style tomatoes, drained & diced
1 cup mozzarella cheese, shredded

Instructions:
Coat large skillet with cooking spray and place on medium-high heat. Add chops and vegetable. Cook 2 minutes or until bottoms of chops are browned. Turn chops over.

Sprinkle with oregano and drizzle with dressing. Cover with tomatoes. Bring to boil and cover. Simmer on low heat 15 minutes or until chops are done, stirring occasionally. Sprinkle with cheese.

Serves 4.

MINI MEAT LOAVES

1 pound ground beef
6 ounces stuffing mix
¼ cup ketchup
1 tablespoon sugar
1 teaspoon garlic powder
1 (15 oz.) can tomato sauce

Instructions:
Preheat oven to 350°F. Mix beef, Stuffing, garlic, and tomato sauce in large bowl.

Press evenly into 12 medium muffin cups sprayed with cooking spray. Bake 30 minutes or until meat loaves are cooked through. Top with ketchup mixture. Bake 10 more minutes. Let stand 10 minutes before serving.

Serves 4.

OXTAIL RAGOUT

4 pounds oxtails, cut crosswise in 2-inch pieces
1 can (10 ½ oz.) condensed beef broth, undiluted
8 small carrots, pared and cut in 1 1/2 -inch pieces (1 ½ lb.)
12 new potatoes, washed and partially pared (1 ½ Ib.)
¼ teaspoon whole black peppers
2 ½ teaspoons salt
1 cup red burgundy
1 cup celery, chopped
1 cup onions, chopped
1 clove garlic, crushed
½ package (10-oz.) frozen peas
¼ cup all-purpose flour
1 cup carrots, chopped
¼ cup butter
2 bay leaves
1 teaspoon thyme leaves, dried

Instructions:

Day before serving: Wash oxtails under cold running water. Wipe dry with paper towels. In hot butter in 5-quart Dutch oven, brown oxtails on all sides, half at a time.

Remove as they are browned to fat. In Dutch oven, add chopped vegetables, garlic, peppers, salt, thyme, and bay leaves; sauté over medium heat, stirring 5 minutes, until onions are golden. Add oxtails, beef broth, and 3 cups water; simmer over low heat, covered, 3 hours, or until oxtails are fork-tender. Let cool to room temperature. Refrigerate, covered overnight.

Next day: With metal spoon, skim off fat from surface and discard.

About 1 hour before serving, add red wine to oxtails, mix well. Heat slowly over low heat, stirring occasionally. Add carrots and potatoes; simmer, covered, 30 minutes, until vegetables are tender. Cook peas as label directs; drain. In small bowl, blend together flour and ½ cup water. Stir into bubbling liquid in Dutch oven; simmer, stirring occasionally, until thickened; about 5 minutes. Sprinkle top with peas.

Serves 4.

SWEET AND SOUR POT ROAST

1 tablespoon oil
1 (4lb) chuck or rump roast
1 can (10.5 oz.) beef bouillon
1 can (16 oz.) jellied cranberry sauce
1 (5 oz.) bottle prepared horseradish
8 carrots peeled and cut into 2 inch pieces
2 onions, quartered

Instructions:
Preheat oven to 350°F. Heat oil in Dutch and brown roast. Whisk together well the bouillon, cranberry sauce and horseradish.

Then pour mixture over meat. Cover and bake for 90 minutes. Add carrots and onions to roast. Recover with foil and bake an additional 90 minutes.

Serves 4.

VEAL PARMESAN

½ cup bread crumbs, dry
2 cup Parmesan cheese, grated
1 teaspoon oregano leaves, dried
1 teaspoon salt
1 cup Rhine wine or dry white Italian wine
⅛ teaspoon pepper
2 eggs, beaten
¾ cup olive oil
2 pounds veal cutlets, sliced ½ inched thick

Instructions:
Combine bread crumbs, cheese, oregano, Salt, and Pepper on waxed Paper; set aside. Wipe veal with damp paper towels. Cut into Serving-size pieces, Pound very thin (⅛ inch thick), using mallet or edge of plate. Dip veal into beaten eggs in shallow dish or pie plate, then into crumbs mixture, coating well on both sides. Slowly heat oil in large, heavy skillet. Sauté cutlets, a few at a time, until golden brown; about 3 minutes on each Side. Remove to heated platter; keep warm. Drain fat from skillet.

Stir in wine, and bring to boiling, stirring to dissolve browned bits in pan. Pour over veal.

PASTA

NOODLES WITH PESTO SAUCE

1 cup olive oil
1 cup chopped parsley, packed
1 tablespoon Basil leaves, dried
¼ cup walnuts or whole pine nuts, finely chopped
2 cloves garlic, crushed
2 tablespoons boiling water
¾ cup Parmesan cheese, grated
1 teaspoon salt
⅛ teaspoon white pepper
2 tablespoons butter
1 package (8 oz.) thin spaghetti or noodles, cooked as package label direct

Instructions:

In small bowl, combine all ingredients except spaghetti. Beat with fork to combine thoroughly. Place well-drained hit spaghetti in large bowl. Pour sauce over Spaghetti and toss lightly to coat thoroughly. Serve with additional Parmesan cheese, if desired.

PIES

BLACKBERRIES COBBLER

4 cups blackberries, frozen
1 tablespoon lemon juice
1 large egg
1 cinnamon sugar for sprinkling
1 cup sugar
1 cup flour
6 tablespoons butter, melted

Instructions:
Preheat oven 375°F. Place berries in a lightly greased 8-inch baking dish. Sprinkle with lemon juice. Stir together egg, sugar and flour in medium bowl until mixture resembles coarse meal. Sprinkle over fruit.

Drizzle melted butter over topping. Bake 45 minutes until lightly browned and bubbly. Sprinkle with cinnamon Sugar. Let stand 10 minutes. Serve warm with sweetened whipped cream or vanilla ice cream if desired.

Serves 4.

BLUEBERRY COBBLER

6 tablespoons unsalted butter
1 cup all-purpose flour
2 teaspoons baking powder
½ teaspoon nutmeg, freshly grated
⅔ cup milk
2 cups blueberries
½ teaspoon salt
1 cup sugar

Instructions:
Recommended: whipped cream or vanilla ice cream.

Preheat oven to 375°F. In an 8-inch baking dish melt butter. Into a bowl sift together flour, baking powder, salt and nutmeg and stir in sugar until combined well. Add milk and whisk batter until it is just combined.

Pour batter into melted butter. Do not stir. Pour berries into center of batter. Do not stir. Bake cobbler in middle of oven 40 minutes, or until cake portion is golden and berries exude juices. Serve cobbler warm or at room temperature with whipped cream or ice cream.

Serves 4.

BUTTERSCOTCH PECAN PIE

3 eggs, sliced
1 cup light corn syrup
⅛ teaspoon salt
1 teaspoon vanilla extract
1 cup light brown sugar
2 tablespoons butter, melted
1 cup pecan or walnut halves
1 9-inch unbaked pie shell
1 whipped cream

Instructions:

Preheat oven to 400°F. In medium bowl, beat eggs slightly. Add corn syrup, salt, vanilla, brown sugar, and butter; mix well.

Stir in nuts. Pour into unbaked pie shell. Bake 15 minutes. Reduce heat to 350°F and bake additional 30 minutes, or until outer edge of filling seems set.

Let cool completely on wire rack. Just before serving, decorate around edge with rosettes of whipped cream.

Serves 4.

CHOCOLATE CREAM PIE

⅓ cup cornstarch
¾ cup sugar
1 9-inch baked pie shell
3 egg yolks, slightly beaten
½ teaspoon vanilla extract
2 ½ cups milk
½ teaspoon salt
2 squares unsweetened chocolate, cut-up

Instructions:
CREAM TOPPING

1 cup heavy cream, 2 tablespoons confectioners' sugar; ½ teaspoon vanilla extract.

In top of double boiler: combine sugar, cornstarch, chocolate, and salt; mix well.

Gradually stir in milk. Cook over boiling water, stirring, until mixture is thickened; about 10 minutes, Cook, covered but stirring occasionally; 10 minutes longer. Gradually stir half the hot mixture into beaten egg yolks; return to double boiler. Cook over boiling water,

Stirring occasionally, 5 minutes. Remove from heat.

Stir in vanilla. Pour chocolate filling into baked pie shell, Refrigerate at least 3 hours, until well chilled. Make cream topping 1 hour before serving; with rotary beater, beat cream confectioners' sugar and vanilla until stiff. Spread over pie. Refrigerate

Serves 4.

DUTCH APPLE PIE

¾ cup all-purpose flour
½ cup light brown sugar
⅓ cup butter
2 pounds tart apples
1 tablespoon lemon juice
2 tablespoons flour
¾ cup sugar
1 dash salt
1 teaspoon cinnamon

Instructions:
Prepare pie shell, and refrigerate until ready to use. Make topping: TOPPING; ¾ cup unsifted all-purpose flour, ½ cup light brown sugar, firmly packed, ⅓ cup butter.

FILLING; 2 Ib. tart apples; 1 tablespoon lemon juice; 2 tablespoons flour: ¾ cup Sugar, dash salt; 1 teaspoon cinnamon.

Prepare pie shell, and refrigerate until ready to use. Make topping; combine flour and sugar in medium bowl. With pastry blender or 2 knives, cut in butter until mixture is consistency of coarse cornmeal.

Refrigerate. Preheat oven to 400°F. Make filling: Core and pare apples. Slice thinly into large bowl. Sprinkle with lemon juice.

Combine flour, sugar, Salt, and cinnamon, mixing well. Toss lightly with apples. Turn filling into unbaked pie shell, spreading evenly. Cover with topping. Bake 40 to 50 minutes, or until apples are tender.

Serves 4.

EASY CHICKEN POT PIE

2 tablespoons Italian salad dressing
2 cups frozen mixed vegetables
1 can (10.75) cream of chicken soup
¼ pound (4 oz.) Velveeta cut into ½ cubes
1 sheet frozen puff pastry, thawed
1 egg, beaten
1 pound chicken, cooked & diced

Instructions:
Preheat oven to 400°F.

Combine chicken, dressing, vegetable, and soup in a medium bowl. Spoon into greased 9-inch square baking dish. Top with Velveeta. Unfold pastry sheet and place over chicken mixture. Fold under edges of Pastry. Press onto top of baking dish to seal. Brush pastry with egg. Cut several slits in pastry to permit steam to escape.

Place on baking sheet. Bake 30 minutes or until crust is deep golden brown. Let stand 5 minutes before serving.

Serves 4.

FETA CHEESE PIE

19-inch unbaked pie shell
¾ pound feta cheese, cut in small pieces
1 cup light cream
3 eggs
½ teaspoon thyme leaves, dried
1 pimientos, cut in strips
1 teaspoon cornstarch
1 dash pepper
1 small garlic cloves, crushed
9 large pitted ripe olives
7 large green olives, pitted

Instructions:

Preheat oven to 425°F. Prick crust well with folk. Place in freeze 10 minutes. Bake pie shell 10 minutes; cool. Blend cheese in electric blender with cream and eggs until smooth. Add thyme, cornstarch, and Pepper, blend. Stir in garlic. Turn into pie Shell. Bake pie 10 minutes. Arrange olives over top. Bake 25 minutes longer, or until filling is set. Decorate with pimiento strips just before serving. Serve warm.

Serves 4.

FRESH BLUEBERRY PIE

1 package pie crust mix
2 pints fresh blueberries
1 tablespoon lemon juice
1 cup sugar
¼ cup all-purpose flour
¼ teaspoon cinnamon
⅛ teaspoon nutmeg
1 dash ground cloves
2 tablespoons butter
1 egg yolk

Instructions:

Prepare pie crust mix as package label directs. Shape into ball; divide in half. On lightly floured surface, roll out half of pastry into 11-inch circle. Use to line 9-inch pie plate. Refrigerate with rest of pastry until to use. Preheat oven to 400°F. Gently wash berries; drain well. Place in large bowl.

Sprinkle with lemon juice. Combine sugar, flour, cinnamon, nutmeg, and cloves. Add to berries; toss lightly to combine. Turn into pastry-lined pie plate, mounding in center.

Dot with butter. Roll out remaining pastry into 11-inch circle. Make several slits near center, for steam vents. Adjust over filling; fold edge of top crust under bottom crust, press together, and crimp decoratively.

Beat egg yolk with tablespoon water. Brush lightly over top crust. Bake 50 minute or until juices start to bubble through steam vents and crust is golden brown. Cool on wire rack at least 1 hours before serving.

POULTRY

BREAST OF CHICKEN PAPRIKA

6 whole chicken breasts
4 tablespoons butter
1 pound small white onions
1 cup onions, chopped
8 small carrots
2 cups sour cream
2 cans (10 ¾ oz.) condensed chicken broth
2 tablespoons paprika
2 teaspoons salt
⅓ cup flour
½ cup white wine, dry

Instructions:

Wash chicken breasts well; pat dry with paper towels. Cut each in half; remove skin, and discard. Brown chicken pieces, half at a time, in 2 tablespoons hot butter in large, heavy skillet or Dutch oven. Remove as browned. In same skillet, sauté whole and chopped onions in remaining 2 tablespoons butter until lightly browned.

Cut carrots into 1 ½ inch pieces. Add to onions; sauté 1 or 2 minutes. Add undiluted chicken broth, paprika, and salt.

Return chicken to skillet, overlapping pieces. Bring to boiling; reduce heat, and simmer, covered, 15 minutes. Rearrange chicken so top pieces are on bottom, for more cooking. Simmer covered, 25 minutes longer, or until chicken is tender.

Remove chicken pieces to larger freezer container. In small bowl, blend flour with wine to make smooth paste. Stir into hot liquid until smooth; (you should have about 3 ½ cups liquid.) Bring to boiling, Stirring; reduce heat, and simmer, 2 minutes. Pour Sauce over chicken. Cool quickly; freezer wrap; freeze. To serve: Thaw in refrigerator overnight. Place chicken and sauce in large skillet or Dutch oven; reheat gently. Remove chicken to warm platter.

Slowly stir sour cream into gravy; heat gently 2 minutes, but do not boil.

Serves 4.

CHICKEN AND NOODLES

1 pound chicken
1 can (26 oz.) cream of chicken soup
1 package egg noodles
3 bouillon cube, cubed
salt and pepper to taste

Instructions:
Boil chicken in water. When chicken is done; take out of pot and save water. Use this water as a starter. Add cream of chicken soup, noodles, and bouillon to water. Cut up chicken and add to pot. Cook until the noodles are done. Add salt and pepper to taste.

Serves 4.

CHICKEN CACCIATORE

2 broiler-fryers, cut-up
3 tablespoons olive oil
2 tablespoons butter
1 can tomato sauce
1 whole tomatoes, canned, un-drained
¾ cup red wine, dry
1 teaspoon oregano leaves, dried
¼ teaspoon garlic, minced
2 tablespoons parsley, chopped
½ teaspoon salt
¼ teaspoon pepper
3 tablespoons flour
1 can (6 oz.) whole mushrooms, drained
1 teaspoon basil, dried

Instructions:

Day before serving: wash chicken, pat dry with paper towels. Heat oil and butter in 6-quart Dutch oven. Add chicken, a few pieces at a time, and brown well on all sides. Remove as browned. Return chicken to Dutch oven. Add tomato sauce, tomatoes, wine, basil, oregano, garlic, parsley, salt, and pepper. Simmer, covered, 45 minutes, or until chicken is tender.

Combine flour with 3 tablespoons water. Stir into sauce. Add mushrooms, and cook 10 minutes longer, or until sauce is thickened. Cool quickly, then cover, and refrigerate overnight. To serve: reheat over low heat.

Serves 4.

CHICKEN LASAGNA

3 cups chicken, cooked & diced
1 small onion, diced
1 (2.25 oz.) can sliced black olives
12 lasagna noodles, prepared
2 (10.75) cream of chicken soup
½ teaspoon garlic powder
¾ cup sour cream
3 cups cheddar cheese, shredded
¾ cup Parmesan cheese

Instructions:
Preheat oven to 350°F. Mix the first 7 ingredients in a bowl. In a 9x13 dish, layer 4 noodles, then half the chicken mix and 1 cup of cheese. Repeat for second layer.

For final layer, use the remaining 4 noodles and remaining 1 cup cheese. Bake uncovered for 45 minutes.

Serves 4.

CHICKEN WITH ARTICHOKE HEARTS AND MUSHROOMS

4 cups pasta, cooked
3 boneless, skinless chicken breast
1 (6 oz.) jar roasted red peppers
1 (6 oz.) jar marinated artichoke hearts
¾ cup chicken broth, reduced fat & low sodium
1 teaspoon dried parsley
3 cups sliced mushrooms
½ cup dry white wine
1 tablespoon cornstarch
salt and pepper to taste

Instructions:
Drain liquid from artichokes into large non-stick skillet and heat over high heat.

Add chicken and brown on all sides. Reduce heat, add mushrooms and cook 10 minutes or until chicken is no longer pink.

Drain red peppers and discard liquid. Coarsely chop artichokes and red peppers, then add to chicken. Combine broth, wine and cornstarch and mix well. Add broth mixture to chicken mixture and increase heat to high; heat to boil. Reduce heat and simmer for 5 minutes or until most of the liquid is absorbed. Toss with pasta, salt and pepper to taste, sprinkle with parsley and serve.

Serves 4.

CRANBERRY CHICKEN

4 chicken breasts, boneless & skinless
8 ounces French salad dressing
1 (16 oz.) can cranberry sauce
1 package dry onion soup mix

Instructions:
Preheat oven to 350°F. In a sealable bag, mix the dressing, soup mix and cranberry sauce. Add chicken. Place mixture in a well-greased baking pan. Bake for 90 minutes, uncovered.

Serve 4.

CURRY-GLAZED FILLET OF SOLE

4 sole fillets
1 teaspoon instant minced onion
¼ cup mayonnaise, low-calorie
¼ cup imitation sour cream
½ teaspoon curry powder

Instructions:
Preheat oven to 500°F. Wash fillets; dry with paper towels. Arrange, in single layer and slightly overlapping, in greased, shallow baking dish. In small bowl, mix mayonnaise, sour cream, onion, and curry powder. Spread mixture evenly over sole.

Bake, uncovered, 15 minutes, or until fish flakes easily and sauce starts to brown.

Garnish with stuffed mushrooms (see stuffed mushrooms recipe).

Serves 4.

EASY CHICKEN POT PIE

2 tablespoons Italian salad dressing
2 cups frozen mixed vegetables
1 can (10.75) cream of chicken soup
¼ pound (4 oz.) Velveeta cut into ½ cubes
1 sheet frozen puff pastry, thawed
1 egg, beaten
1 pound chicken, cooked & diced

Instructions:
Preheat oven to 400°F. Combine chicken, dressing, vegetable, and soup in a medium bowl. Spoon into greased 9-inch square baking dish. Top with Velveeta. Unfold pastry sheet and place over chicken mixture. Fold under edges of pastry. Press onto top of baking dish to seal. Brush pastry with egg. Cut several slits in pastry to permit steam to escape. Place on baking sheet. Bake 30 minutes or until crust is deep golden brown. Let stand 5 minutes before serving.

Serves 4.

ORANGE CHICKEN STIR FRY

2 tablespoons oil
4 chicken breasts, boneless & skinless, cut in strips
⅛ teaspoon pepper
½ cup cashew pieces
2 tablespoons soy sauce
1 tablespoon cornstarch
2 cups frozen baby peas, thawed
¼ teaspoon salt
¾ cup orange juice

Instructions:
Heat oil in heavy skillet or wok. Add chicken, salt and pepper. Stir fry until chicken is cooked, 5 minutes. Combine orange juice, soy sauce and cornstarch in small bowl. Add to chicken in skillet or wok along with frozen peas. Stir fry 5 minutes until thickens. Stir in cashew pieces and serve over hot cooked rice or noodles.

Serves 4.

ROASTED WHOLE CHICKEN

1 whole chicken
1 onion powder
1 garlic powder
1 roasting bags
1 butter
salt and pepper to taste

Instructions:
Take chicken out of packaging, making sure there are no parts inside. If so, remove. Rub chicken with butter, sprinkle with seasoning. Follow direction in roasting bag. Bake for about 60 minutes.

Serves 4.

SWEET POTATO CHICKEN SKILLET

4 boneless, skinless chicken breast
2 medium sweet potatoes, cut into
8 wedges each
3 tablespoons olive oil
2 tablespoons Caribbean Citrus spice blend

Instructions:
Heat a cast iron skillet to medium heat. Add 1 ½ tablespoon olive oil. Toss in sweet potatoes and brown on all sides for 1 minutes. Remove to a plate.

Add remaining olive oil and brown chicken on both sides. Return sweet potatoes to pan and sprinkle all with Caribbean Citrus spice blend. Cook 3 minutes, toss and serve.

SALADS

APPLE AND BASIL CHICKEN SALAD

4 boneless, skinless chicken breast
4 teaspoons kosher salt
1 teaspoon black pepper
¼ cup fresh lime juice
4 scallions, thinly sliced
2 granny smith apples, diced
⅓ cup roasted peanuts, roughly chopped
2 tablespoons fresh mint, thinly sliced
1 tablespoon white wine vinegar
2 tablespoons light brown sugar
½ cup fresh basil, thinly sliced

Instructions:
Pat the chicken dry with paper towels and pound to an even thinness. Place the chicken in a large saucepan and add enough water to cover by ½ inch. Add 3 teaspoons of the salt and ½ teaspoons of the pepper and bring to a gentle simmer.

Cook 10 minutes. Transfer the chicken to a bowl of ice water for 5 minutes. Meanwhile, in a large bowl, combine the lime juice, vinegar, and sugar, stirring until the sugar dissolves. Add the scallions and apples and toss. Drain the chicken and pat it dry. Dice the chicken and add it to the apple mixture along with the peanuts, mint, basil, and the remaining salt and pepper. Toss and divide among individual plates.

Serves 4.

BROCCOLI SALAD

⅓ pound bacon, cooked and crumbled
½ cup low fat yogurt
¼ cup mayonnaise
2 tablespoons sugar
1 tablespoon lemon juice
3 cups broccoli florets
½ teaspoon ground black pepper
½ cup red onions, chopped
¼ cup sunflower seeds, roasted
½ cup raisins
½ cup feta cheese

Instructions:
Mix everything together except for the bacon. Sprinkle the bacon on top of salad. Cover and refrigerate for 3 hours.

Serves 4.

CAULIFLOWER SALAD BOWL

4 cups raw cauliflower, thinly sliced
⅔ cup green peppers, coarsely chopped
½ cup onions, chopped
½ cup pimientos, coarsely chopped

Instructions:
DRESSING: ½ cup Olive oil; 3 tablespoons lemon juice; 1 tablespoons wine vinegar; 2 teaspoons salt; 1 tablespoon sugar; ¼ teaspoon pepper.

In medium bowl, combine cauliflower, olives, green pepper, pimiento, and onion.

Make dressing: In small bowl, combine olive oil, lemon juice, vinegar, salt, sugar, and pepper. Beat with rotary beater until well blended. Pour over cauliflower mixture.

Refrigerate, covered, until well chilled about 4 hours or overnight.

To serve: Spoon salad into bowl lined with salad greens. Toss just before serving.

Serves 4.

CHEF'S SALAD BOWL

½ bottle low-calorie oil and vinegar-type dressing
2 tablespoons mayonnaise, low-calorie
1 crisp salad greens, shredded in bite-size pieces (1 ½ quart)
2 tablespoons fresh chives, snipped
2 cups slivered cooked tongue (1/4 lbs)
1 ½ cups slivered cooked chicken (1/2 lbs)
¼ pound natural Swiss cheese, slivered
1 medium tomato, cut in 8 wedges

Instructions:

In a small bowl, combine dressing with mayonnaise. With wire whisk or rotary beater, beat well. Refrigerate, covered. Just before serving, place greens and chives in salad bowl. Add tongue, chicken and cheese. Stir dressing well. Pour over salad; toss to coat meat and greens. Garnish with tomato wedges.

Serves 4.

CRAB SALAD

2 cans (7 ¾ oz.) king crab meat, drained
½ cup mayonnaise, low-calorie
2 tablespoons parsley, chopped
1 teaspoon Worcestershire sauce
1 teaspoon lemon juice
2 tablespoons chives, snipped
4 hard cooked eggs, quartered
1 cup cucumber crisp lettuce cups, diced and pared

Instructions:

If necessary, remove cartilage from crab meat. In medium bowl, combine mayonnaise, parsley, chives, Worcestershire, and lemon juice. Mix well. Add crab meat and cucumber; toss. Refrigerate, covered, until well chilled, about 1 hour. To serve, arrange lettuce cups on 4 serving plates. Fill with salad; garnish with eggs.

Serves 4.

MACARONI SALAD

1 cup elbow macaroni
½ cup cucumbers, diced and unpared
2 tablespoons sweet pickle relish
1 ½ teaspoons onions, grated
1 hard cooked eggs, chopped
¼ cup mayonnaise
¼ cup sour cream
2 tablespoons milk
½ teaspoon salt
1 dash pepper
¼ cup green peppers, diced

Instructions:
Cook macaroni as package label directs. Drain, then rinse with cold water. Place in large bowl.

Add cucumber, green pepper, pickle relish, and grated onion, mix well. In small bowl, combine mayonnaise, sour cream, milk, salt, and pepper, blend well. Pour over macaroni mixture; toss until macaroni is well coated. Gently mix in chopped egg.

Refrigerate, covered, until well chilled, several hours or overnight. To serve: Garnish with green pepper strips, if desired.

Serves 4.

QUICK CHICKEN CURRY SALAD

1 rotisserie chicken, meat and skin removed, chopped
2 hard cooked eggs, chopped
½ cup mayonnaise
½ cup apples, chopped
½ cup celery, chopped
¼ cup onions, chopped
2 teaspoons curry powder
1 teaspoon paprika
½ teaspoon cayenne pepper
salt to taste

Instructions:
Mix the chicken, eggs, mayonnaise, apple, celery, curry powder, paprika, cayenne pepper, and salt in a large bowl. Cover and refrigerate for 60 minutes before serving.

Serves 4.

SOUR CREAM AND APPLE COLESLAW

1 ½ cups sour cream
1 teaspoon salt
2 quarts green cabbage, finely shredded
1 cup tart red apples, cubed and unpared
3 tablespoons lemon juice
½ teaspoon paprika
4 teaspoons pepper

Instructions:

Mix sour cream in medium bowl. Add rest of ingredients, except cabbage and apples; mix well. Pour dressing over cabbage and apples; toss well until coated. Refrigerate at least 30 minutes.

Serves 4.

SUPER EASY SALAD BOWL

6 medium potatoes
1 medium onion
1 bottle (8 oz.) Italian salad dressing, low-cal
1 iceberg lettuce, washed
1 can (7 ¾ oz.) salmon
1 tablespoon fresh dill, chopped
1 can (7 oz.) solid pack tuna, without oil

Instructions:
Scrub potatoes. Cook in boiling salted water, covered, just until tender (about 30 minutes. Drain; let cool slightly. Peel potatoes; cut into slices, ¼ inch thick. Peel onion; slice, and separate into rings. In shallow baking dish, arrange potato slices and onion rings in alternate layers. Add ¾ cup dressing. Refrigerate, covered, 3 hours. Meanwhile, drain tuna and salmon.

Break into large chunks; remove any bone and skin from salmon. Break into large chunks; toss with remaining dressing.

Refrigerate, covered. To serve:

In shallow serving dish, arrange potato and onion in layers, alternately with fish mixture. Sprinkle dill over top. Garnish with lettuce.

Serves 4.

SWEET CHICKEN SALAD

2 poached boneless chicken breasts, diced
1 teaspoon rosemary
1 bay leaf
1 cup celery, diced
1 cup seedless white grapes: diced
½ cup pecans or almonds, chopped
½ cup slaw dressing
salt and pepper to taste

Instructions:

Place chicken breasts in bottom of a small, heavy-bottomed pot. They should fit in a single layer but fit quite snugly. Cover chicken with broth or water. Add rosemary and bay leaf. Bring to a boil, then quickly reduce heat to low so that the water is barely at a simmer. Partly cover and gently simmer for 10 minutes. Turn off heat completely, and allow chicken to remain in hot water for 20 minutes. Remove from pot and let chicken cool. Dice chicken. Mix all ingredients and chill for 24 hours.

Serves 4.

THAI CUCUMBER SALAD

3 large cucumbers
3 cups rice wine vinegar
2 tablespoons sugar
roasted red pepper flakes to taste
cilantro to taste

Instructions:
Cube cucumbers and add other ingredients in a glass or plastic bowl, allow to blend in refrigerator for 5 hours for best flavour and texture. Add fresh cilantro.

Serves 4.

WALDORF SUMMER CHICKEN SALAD

1 pound (2 oz.) red apples, diced
1 cup light mayonnaise
4 shallots, sliced
1 cup walnuts, chopped
1 romaine lettuce
1 sliced apple and walnuts, to garnish
3 tablespoons fresh lemon juice
1 cup celery
2 cloves garlic, crushed
1 pound (2 oz.) cooked chicken, cubed
1 pepper

Instructions:
Place the apples in a bowl with the lemon juice and 1 tablespoon of mayonnaise.

Leave for 40 minutes. Using a sharp knife, slice the celery very thinly. Add the celery, shallots, garlic and walnuts to the apple and mix well. Stir in the remaining mayonnaise and blend well. Add the cooked chicken to the bowl and mix well. Line a glass salad bowl or serving dish with lettuce leaves.

Pile the chicken salad into the center, sprinkle with pepper and garnish with the apple slices and walnuts.

Serves 4.

ZUCCHINI TOSSED SALAD

1 small romaine lettuce
3 medium zucchini, washed and thinly sliced
1 cup radishes, sliced
1 small Boston lettuce, sliced
3 tablespoons green onions, sliced

Instructions:
GARLIC DRESSING: ¼ cup olive oil; 3 tablespoon tarragon vinegar;
2 teaspoon salt; 1 clove garlic, crushed ⅛ teaspoon black pepper.

Wash, dry, and chill salad greens. In large bowl, toss zucchini, radishes,
and onion. Refrigerate, covered; about 1 hour. In jar with tight-fitting
lid, combine all ingredients for garlic dressing. Shake well and chill.
At serving time, tear romaine, and lettuce into bite-size pieces. Add to
vegetables in bowl.

Add garlic dressing, toss until greens and vegetables are well coated.
Serve as a first course salad, or in menus suggesting a green salad.

SEAFOOD

CORN OYSTERS

2 eggs, separated
1 can (12 oz.) whole kernel corn, drained
⅛ teaspoon Worcestershire sauce
¼ teaspoon baking powder
¼ cup all-purpose flour, sifted
1 salad oil
½ teaspoon salt
¼ teaspoon black pepper

Instructions:

In small bowl, with portable electric mixer, beat egg whites until stiff but not dry; set aside. In another bowl, beat egg yolks slightly. Add com, Worcestershire, salt and pepper, combine thoroughly. Stir in flour and baking powder. Fold in beaten egg whites. Heat about 2 teaspoons oil in large skillet over medium heat. Drop corn mixture by tablespoonsful into hot oil and brown; about 3 minutes on each side.

Remove and keep hot while cooking remaining mixture, adding more oil as needed.

Serves 4.

EASY CEVICHE

1 package imitation crab meat
1 cup chopped tomatoes
½ cup green peppers
2 lemons
1 package shrimp
1 cup cucumbers, chopped
1 teaspoon hot sauce
salt and pepper to taste

Instructions:
In large bowl, place crab meat and cooked shrimp, mix well together. Add the juice of the lemons. Then add the rest of the ingredients. Mix well. Put in Refrigerator for 3 hours before serving.

Serves 4.

SOUPS

CHICKEN AND LEEK SOUP

1 pound chicken, boneless
2 tablespoons butter
1 bouquet garni sachet
1 pound leeks
5 cups chicken stock
8 prunes, pitted
1 red bell peppers, diced
rice, cooked
salt and pepper to taste

Instructions:

Using a sharp knife, cut the chicken and leeks unto 1-inch pieces. Melt the butter in a large saucepan, add the chicken and leeks and fry for 8 minutes, stirring occasionally. Add the chicken stock and bouquet garni sachet to the mixture in the pan, and season with salt and pepper to taste. Bring the soup to the boil and simmer over a gentle heat for 45 minutes.

Add the pitted prunes with some cooked rice and diced red bell peppers, and simmer for 20 minutes. Remove the bouquet garni sachet and discard. Pour the soup into a warm tureen or individual bowls and serve.

Serves 4.

COUNTRY CHICKEN CHOWDER

2 tablespoons butter flavoured Crisco
1 medium onions, chopped
2 cans (10 ¾ oz.) condensed noodle soup
2 cups cooked chicken, diced
2 tablespoons chopped parsley
1 can (15 oz.) cream-style corn
1 cup water
1 can (5 oz.) evaporated milk
½ teaspoon white pepper

Instructions:

Melt butter flavoured Crisco in large saucepan on medium heat. Add onion. Sauté until soft. Stir in soup, chicken, corn, water, evaporated milk and pepper. Bring to a boil. Reduce heat. Simmer 10 minutes.

Serve sprinkled with parsley.

Serves 4.

OXTAIL SOUP

3 pounds oxtail, cut-up
3 tablespoons butter
1 can (10 ½ oz.) condensed beef consommé
2 teaspoons salt
2 teaspoons Worcestershire sauce
1 teaspoon dried thyme
1 teaspoon dried tarragon
6 whole black peppers
1 parsley, chopped
1 bay leaves
1 clove garlic, crushed
1 egg
2 cups white turnip, diced
1 ½ cups carrots, pared
1 ½ cups celery, sliced
1 cup onions, chopped
½ cup claret

Instructions:
Wipe oxtail with damp paper towels. In hot butter in 6-quart kettle, slowly brown oxtail on all sides; about 30 minutes. Add 2 quarts water, consommé', salt,

Worcestershire, thyme, tarragon, black peppers, bay leaf, and garlic. Bring to boiling; reduce heat, and simmer, covered, 3 ½ hours. Remove from heat. Remove oxtail with slotted spoon, and separate the meat from the bones. Cut the meat into bite-size pieces and return to pot. Add the carrots and celery. Cover and simmer 10 to 15 minutes or until carrots are tender.

SHRIMP AND CRAB SOUP

1 sweet red pepper
1 green pepper
2 carrots, pared
1 whole tomatoes, canned, un-drained
½ teaspoon hot red pepper, dried & crushed
4 whole cloves
2 shallots, peeled
2 cans (10 ¾ oz.) condensed chicken broth, undiluted
1 ½ cups celery, chopped
½ teaspoon basil leaves, dried
⅛ teaspoon thyme leaves, dried
¼ teaspoon turmeric
1 whole bay leaf
1 teaspoon salt
1 white onion, peeled
1 pound fresh shrimp, unshelled
1 can (7 ¾ oz.) king crab meat, drained and cartilage removed
¼ cup lemon juice
1 tablespoon chopped parsley

Instructions:

Wash peppers. Remove ribs and seeds; cut into small pieces. Slice carrots thinly crosswise. (You should have about 1 cup each pepper and carrot.) Break up tomatoes with folk. Stud onion with cloves.

Slice shallots. In large saucepan, bring 3 cups water and chicken broth to boiling. Add red and green pepper, carrot, tomato, onion with cloves, shallot, celery, basil, thyme, turmeric, bay leaf, and dried red pepper. Return to boiling; reduce heat, and simmer uncovered, 30 minutes. Cook shrimp: in small saucepan, bring 2 cups water with salt to boiling. Add shrimp.

Simmer, uncovered, 10 minutes. Drain, reserving 1 cup liquid. Cool shrimp; shell and de vein. Add shrimp, reserved cooking liquid, crab meat, and lemon juice to soup.

Cook gently, uncovered, 10 minutes. Add parsley at end of cooking time. Taste; add salt if desired.

Serves 4.

SPICY POTATO SOUP

1 pound ground beef, cooked & drained
4 cups potatoes, peeled & cubed
1 small onion, chopped
24 ounces tomato sauce
4 cups water
2 teaspoons black pepper
1 ½ teaspoons hot pepper sauce

Instructions:
Combine all ingredients and bring to a boil and then simmer for 60 minutes or until potatoes are tender and soup has thickened.

Serves 4.

VEGETABLES

BROCCOLI WITH LEMON SAUCE

1 bunch broccoli, fresh
6 cups boiling water
salt
¼ cup olive oil
½ cup garlic, finely chopped
2 tablespoons lemon juice

Instructions:
Remove large leaves and tough portions of broccoli. Wash thoroughly; drain. Separate, splitting large stalks into quarters. Place in 6-quart saucepan. Add boiling water and 1 teaspoon salt. Cook, covered, 10 minutes, or until tender; drain in colander. In same pan, place olive oil and garlic; heat until bubbly. Add broccoli; sprinkle with lemon juice and ½ teaspoon salt. Cook, covered, 1 minute, or until broccoli is heated through. Serve hot.

BROCCOLI AMANDINE

1 bunch broccoli, fresh
½ cup boiling water
2 tablespoons lemon juice
½ cup almonds, slivered
¼ cup butter
salt

Instructions:

Wash and trim leaves from broccoli. If stalks are very large, split lengthwise right through flower. Arrange in single layer in bottom of large skillet. Pour boiling water over broccoli; sprinkle with salt. Cook over medium heat, covered, 10 minutes, or until stalks are tender and water is evaporated.

Meanwhile, sauté almonds in tablespoon butter until golden. Add remaining butter and lemon juice. Heat until butter melts.

Pour over broccoli.

Serves 4.

RICE

MEXICAN RICE

⅔ cup onions, chopped
3 tablespoons bacon fat
1 cup raw converted white rice
1 can (8 oz.) whole tomatoes
2 teaspoons salt
1 cup green peppers, chopped
1 teaspoon chili powder

Instructions:
Chopped fresh tomato, and chopped green pepper (optional)

In medium-size heavy skillet with tight-fitting cover, sauté onion in hot bacon fat. Stir in rice, 1 cup green pepper, chili powder, canned tomatoes, and salt. Add 2 cups water. Bring to boiling, then reduce heat, and simmer, covered, 20 minutes, or until liquid is absorbed and rice is cooked.

Garnish with chopped tomato and green pepper.

BEANS

SWEET AND HOT GREEN BEANS

3 (14 oz.) cans green beans
¾ cup brown sugar, packed
2 tablespoons chili powder
10 slices bacon, uncooked & chopped

Instructions:
Preheat oven to 350°F. Grease or spray 9x13 pan. Spread green beans on bottom.

In a bowl, combine brown sugar and chili powder. Sprinkle evenly over. Place bacon over top. Bake for 45 minutes or until bacon is crispy.